Closing Up for Winter

poems by

Jim McDermott

Finishing Line Press
Georgetown, Kentucky

Closing Up for Winter

For
family

Publisher: Leah Maines

Editor: Christen Kincaid

Cover Art: Jim McDermott

Author Photo: Jim McDermott

Cover Design: Elizabeth Maines McCleavy

Printed in the USA on acid-free paper.
Order online: www.finishinglinepress.com
                    also available on amazon.com

Author inquiries and mail orders:
Finishing Line Press
P. O. Box 1626
Georgetown, Kentucky 40324
U. S. A.

Table of Contents

IV. Winter

There Are Always Remnants

"The woods will either have me or they'll send me home."
—*Rick Bass*

There are always
remnants of light

by the window
in the corner

where we set
the space heater
down for the night.

The glow of the old code
it displays and erases

is like the idea
you once had
of being
a writer in the woods—

and even from
across the room

you can nearly feel
what it was like

to move your hands
closer to the heat
of the apparatus
and the harrow

as you served out
your sentence of joy.

I. Spring

Willed

Listening to the
woods drip rain
that stopped
in the night,
and knowing
there's a life
of systems
being tended to
without us.
If someone were there,
under the leaves—
if we just got out of bed
and walked with
each other through
the drenching grass.

Progenitor

I just
want

what
reality

it is:

a line

that's
tender

as an
oak's

mid-
vein.

The Back Hill

It must not hurt
to hear the creek
in the morning.

To time the traces
in small pools
of rusted iron
being washed away

like shape itself

from the bedframe
someone once sent
down the back hill

with cups and
patterned plates.

If you are forced
to leave, leave fast,
and do not sleep

where the water
catches you.

Mountaintop Removal

Reflected
sound of

truck tires
on dry

leaves

is the sound
of

wood frogs—

masked, damp—

small as
thumbnails

that travel together

      crossing

overburden

to reach
the vernal

pools.

Objective

To drink milk
of human kindness
for hangover.

To be awake
on the other side,
like a thief of ashes.

*

How the patriarch
is chained while
the children eat.

How the water
is safe to bathe
in light.

Out

Some buildings
aren't
dwellings.

Some skies
aren't blacker
with birds
than clouds.

       *

The cabin
unhoused
on the
ridge—

no wind
in

the
out kept
out.

II. Summer

My Father Washes with Fels-Naptha

Leaf bits wobbling, just, where the cooler's
buttoned spout drips. Fogged consciousness
of miked crowds—"this is Redskins Radio"—
further blurred as he plunges hands basinward
when a play gets called dead. Now he's lifting all
this slickened skin into the air so the next screen
pass can be heard. Rain swallowing the woods,
woods swallowing rain. Forty-four more years
is the reach he will have through time to wrench
out poison ivy, fill this chipped vessel he keeps
dipping a bar of "solvent" soap into, and quiet
animate water by waiting out its soft career over
the jump and into the bloody kettle, the way the
autumn and our lives in this cabin will be, too.

Tree Litter

Hundred-
year-old

beer
bottle

moss-
ed

enmired

I can't make out
the name of

Orchard

Wasps
with their

hooks
out

a model of

and a

model
for

our world
is just a clammy
jar

we'll never
get
out of

a

drowsed
interior-

ity

a
sci-fi
city

Fourth of July

The cabin's
summer-damp
weight

grounds
the ridge
it's rooted in:

ache of place

Davis Pasture

Dusk sky's
designing
swallows

conduce
to bats

to

thoughts

Vermiculate

By a pine branch
hotly curing

in the creek's
clearest pool

a rattlesnake
attaches itself

with weapons
it conceals

in the roof
of its mouth

to the worm-tracked
flank of a trout.

Fatten at the
table of another.

Walker

Found the crow

it was the
saddest thing

couldn't even

salvage a feather
to sew with

Father and Son

Dark green leaves

on the
road

after a storm.

Mosquitoes

clapped
into smudges

against the skin.

Torn laterals

lashing
back

along the path.

Whoever dared

disturb
this place

has gone.

III. Fall

South Fork Sleepy Creek

Driving to the Unger Store
on a rainy afternoon
in apple season,

you can feel the
propeller wash
and wrenching launch

of orchard trucks
in the oncoming lane.

Those pilots
in their orange
stocking caps:

each old man
with a loosened hand

waving in the updraft

like a Lodi blossom
in the storm.

The Clay-Eaters

Rain melts
the licks,
mineral shapes
Mr. Davis
calls his
"deer beer."
How a hole
in the throat
can bait
the fingers
into speech.

North

My father's eyes
wander

to the Big Dipper's

handle
and bowl.

*

In the neighbor's
A-frame

a stripper from Baltimore

watches *Dynasty*
at night.

*

What we care
about

is what we

leave
behind.

Kitchen

I find
myself

lifting
dead flies

by the wing

clearing
the counters

of forked faces
crude hungers.

How light
were

we?

Bunk Bed Reader

Moth-blurred
light

an

imagined
margin

a doubled

erasure

Chanced

Windshield
       pasted
  with   wet
       leaves.

           Porch
  screen
  like a
    crossword
         after
rain.

      The meadow
  webs that
         can't be
seen
   except when water's
  what they've   caught
  are the
       brains of old
farmers
  lit up   by
     Shake-A-Day
              on winter
mornings
  at the Unger Store.

Each   moment
we
  are lifeless,
          the pot of
                this   world
          seems
  smaller

      like it's   said
    the sky
                does those
            idle
            Januarys.

  Under the
    counter and
                the skin   dirt and light
      collect.

The "Gooder" Road

Ditch pools
yellow with leaves.

Bright culvert
spilling wet stones.

At the end of autumn, I see what's half-expected:

Gate snapped from its post by an ice-loosed pickup.

Dried-up
blackberry vines.

Gravel being changed to dust

dust to untouchable sky.

Posted

A cabin

by
itself

portrays
nothing.

Woods edge

that's
just

irregular
enough.

View the
damage

to the
clearcut

from
the air.

Some Animals

The black
snake

the whippoorwill
in the white pine
by the firepit

Phil's hound
that walked all the way
to the main road

Phil's horse
that bolted
from machine guns

the young copperheads
frozen
in the Davis barn

the deer at the hunting area
with an arrow through
its stomach

the deer that died
when the tree fell across
its back (found by the tramp)

his pose beside it
on the front page
of the *Morgan Messenger*

Road Hunters

Watching the borrow pits
for turkeys
while my father drives,

I see a dead young deer
hanging by its antlers
from the raised-up bucket

of a tractor
that's been parked
inside a machine shed
on a farm.

Stuck on a metal
tooth, the deer
flashes out death news

through
the slim opening
the farmer judged sufficient

to help the fat spikehorn
he'd just shot
to cool before the cleaning.

Deer Camp

They had the idea of driving into town
after the beer had run out, but they had
thrown their car keys into the woods.

They discussed whether to walk.
Or to make us go the eleven miles.

We went to call in crows and lost track
of where they were. Later, we heard them
shouting a woman's name.

It was no one we knew.

Listening, we guessed they were following
a creek. We hoped they had some idea
where it was taking them.

We sat on the little porch,
light from the cabin
catching our faces.

They were out there, like bears
or dogs. We knew that much.
Our fathers were in the woods now.

IV. Winter

Gutting Table

When I was a boy,
my father would
douse the comb
he used on me,
so that I would be
more than presentable—
exaggeratedly neat.
And that's what
the bird's fine down
reminded me of:
Nerves combed, wet,
by the hand of a father.

Museum-Going

I don't imagine
him looking
at one painting
or another.

I just sense
the cold marble,
the quiet spaces,
and his contentment
at being alone.

Looking at a work of art,
one sometimes thinks:
my life is going to change.
At least, that's what
Raymond Carver said.

If my father
ever thought that,
I would bet
he didn't linger
in the uplift.

I would bet he let it go
long before he knew
he would ever really miss it.

Morning in the World

It is always
mourning
in the world

and for it—

always
the sadness
that follows grief

into the inner
dark

where it gets colder
at night
than it ever does here

where "it" means
just what it can
never say

with one eye
closed

the other
shut

Weegee Shot

If a middle-aged man
slowly drinks his own weight

in beer and vodka

does that mean
his body vanishes

for that one
weekend?

What you had to
walk around inside of

didn't seem
that
solid
to begin with—

at least
half liquid.

Next to the television set

between the coffee table
and piano bench

a man in a flannel
shirt
sleeps it off

on the crocheted

round rug that
says "Yellowstone."

Empathy

All that winter
the white-tailed deer
looked in the windows
at night.

Whether they were asking
for some guessed-at fellowship,
or just were being animals
stunned by the porch light
as they crossed the dried-out
meadow, we will never know.

The only life worth wanting
could be someone else's,
not your own.

Buck awake at the glass:
a part, a bone hand.

One Room

The darkness
outside
the cabin.

The cabin
containing
the darkness.

That blackout's
the color

of the knots
in our
woods

of the
"no"
in night's throat.

The weight
the light
unbraces.

Closing Up for Winter

I can almost
imagine

the silence
of the cabin
in winter

the day after
the day

after
the day

we shut
the water
to the pipes

the power
to the
refrigerator

the heat
to the snakes
and our familiar mice—

and turned off, too,
the sources that supply
our land with kindness

and whatever it is
we have to have
to need each other

the way
we need each other
only there

only in the woods

thinking of
the hard freeze
that's sure to come

as we pack up
our bags and
our baggage

stuff our voices
into the duffels
of our soft faces

set our hearts
back down gently
inside their cages

and hide
the key
once more

Shine Forth

Only in

a

clearing

I made

for
myself—

only in

a

work

I
didn't

write.

www.ingramcontent.com/pod-product-compliance
Lightning Source LLC
LaVergne TN
LVHW051608080426
835510LV00020B/3191